What's Inside
Spacecraft

W
FRANKLIN WATTS
LONDON•SYDNEY

Franklin Watts
Published in paperback in 2018 by The Watts Publishing Group

Copyright © 2015 David West Children's Books

Designed and illustrated by David West

Dewey number 629.4'7-dc23
PB ISBN 978 1 4451 6349 9

Printed in Malaysia

Franklin Watts
An imprint of
Hachette Children's Group
Part of The Watts Publishing Group
Carmelite House
50 Victoria Embankment
London EC4Y 0DZ

An Hachette UK Company
www.hachette.co.uk

www.franklinwatts.co.uk

WHAT'S INSIDE SPACECRAFT
was produced for Franklin Watts by
David West ⚇ Children's Books, 6 Princeton Court, 55 Felsham Road, London SW15 1AZ

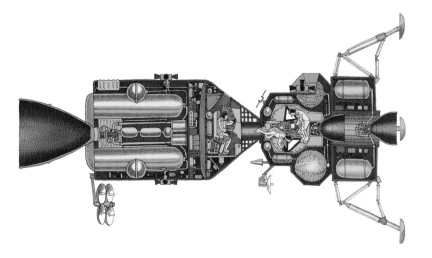

Contents

An **ejector seat** fired Gagarin away from his Vostok 3KA capsule, high above Earth. He then separated from the seat and parachuted to the ground.

Vostok 1

In 1961, Yuri Gagarin, the Russian **cosmonaut**, became the first person to travel into space. The Vostok 1 space flight made one **orbit** around Earth at a height of 169 kilometres (105 miles). The flight took one hour and 48 minutes from launch to landing back on Earth.

Vostok 3KA

Descent capsule

Entry/Escape hatch
This is blown off before the ejector seat is fired.

Porthole

Heat shield
The outer skin of the descent capsule protects it from high temperatures as it hurtles through Earth's atmosphere.

Antenna

Instruments
These show cabin air pressure and temperature as well as the position in orbit above Earth.

Ejector seat
It fires the cosmonaut out of the capsule 7 kilometres (4.3 miles) above Earth's surface.

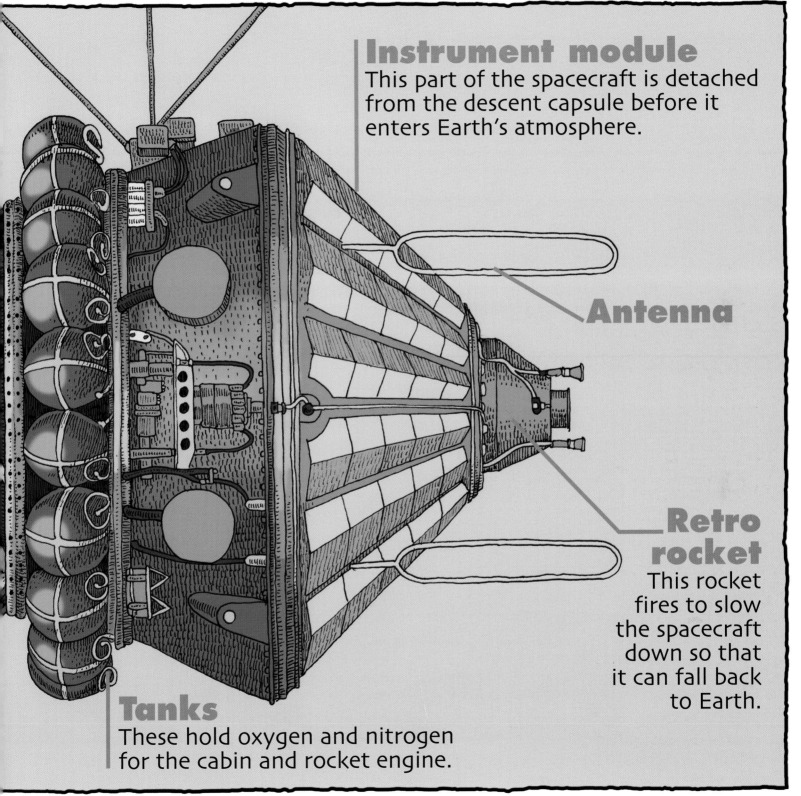

Instrument module
This part of the spacecraft is detached from the descent capsule before it enters Earth's atmosphere.

Antenna

Retro rocket
This rocket fires to slow the spacecraft down so that it can fall back to Earth.

Tanks
These hold oxygen and nitrogen for the cabin and rocket engine.

Moon Landing

In 1969, the US astronauts, Neil Armstrong and Edwin 'Buzz' Aldrin, became the first people to land on the Moon. They spent about two and a half hours walking on the Moon. Michael Collins piloted the command spacecraft in orbit around the Moon until Armstrong and Aldrin returned in the Ascent Module.

All three astronauts travelled to the Moon in the Command Module of Apollo 11. When it was time to land on the Moon, two astronauts entered the Moon lander which they called the 'Eagle'.

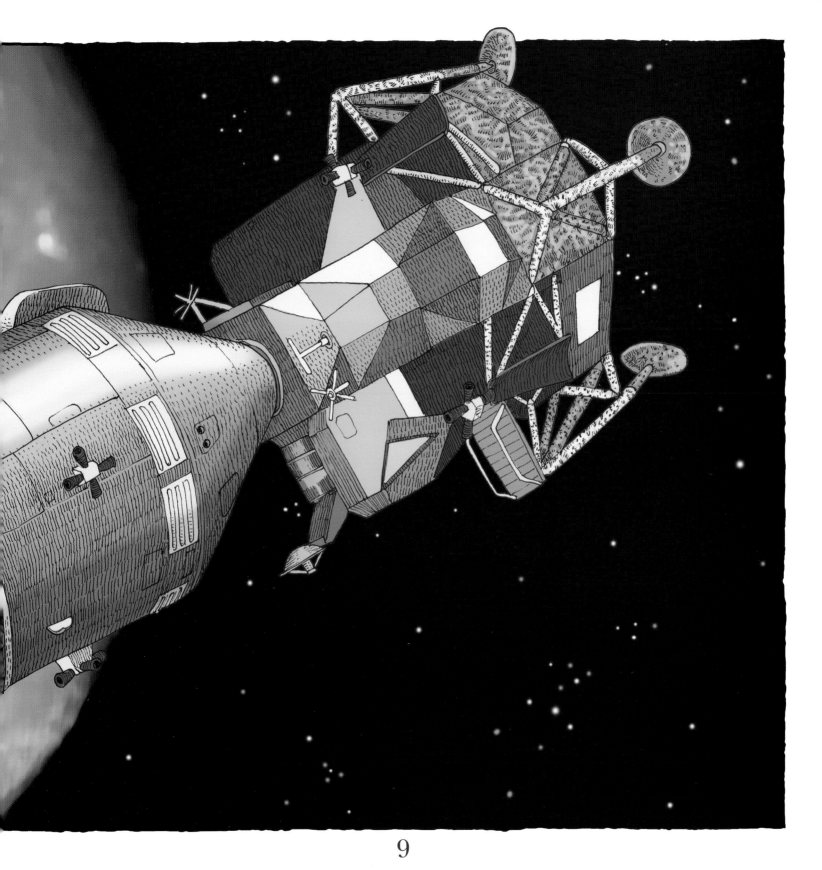

Apollo 11

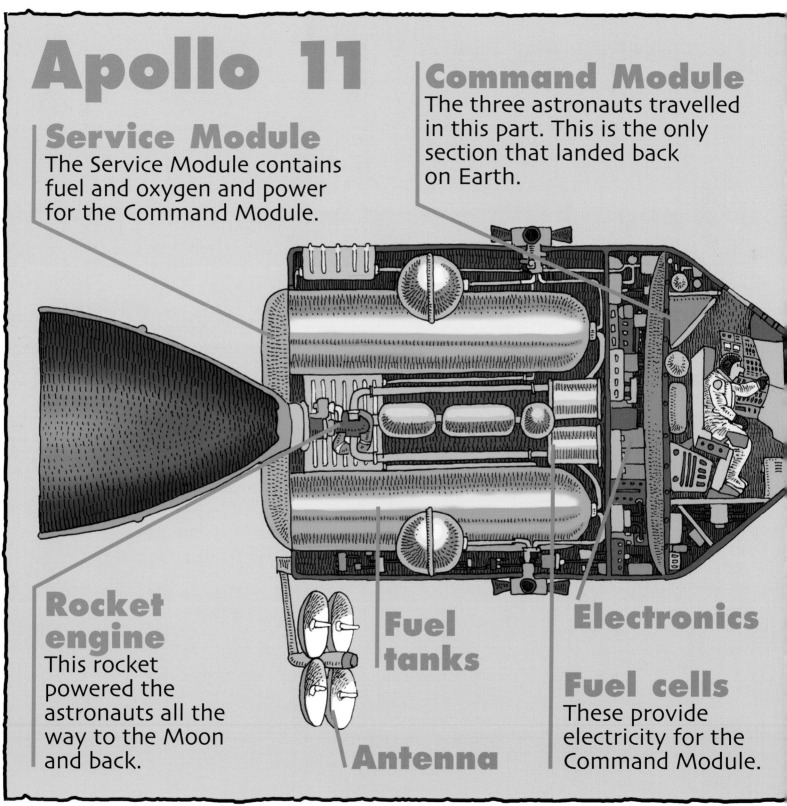

Service Module

The Service Module contains fuel and oxygen and power for the Command Module.

Command Module

The three astronauts travelled in this part. This is the only section that landed back on Earth.

Rocket engine

This rocket powered the astronauts all the way to the Moon and back.

Fuel tanks

Electronics

Fuel cells

These provide electricity for the Command Module.

Antenna

Fuel tanks

Rocket engine

The Eagle

The Moon lander was called the Eagle. It had two parts. The Descent Module, along with the Ascent Module, landed on the Moon. The Ascent Module took off and returned to the Command Module.

Rocket engine

Oxygen tanks

Ascent Module

Two astronauts landed on the Moon. The Ascent Module part of the Eagle then returned to the Command Module.

Descent Module

This part had four legs that touched down on the Moon.

The X-15 could fly into space, which is 100 kilometres (62.1 miles) above sea level. Many pilots flying the X-15 were awarded the astronaut badge.

Rocket Plane

The fastest plane ever was the X-15, which could travel at 7,273 kph (4,519 mph). It was powered by a rocket engine and flew to an altitude of 107.8 kilometres (67 miles). The X-15 was one of many X-planes that tested new materials and designs that were used to build the Space Shuttle.

X-15

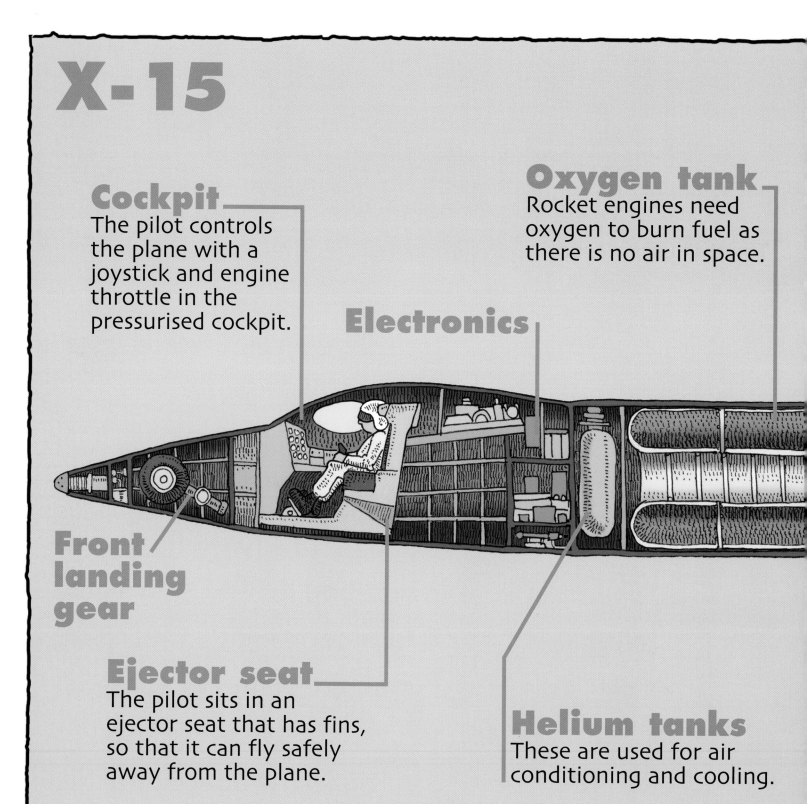

Cockpit
The pilot controls the plane with a joystick and engine throttle in the pressurised cockpit.

Electronics

Oxygen tank
Rocket engines need oxygen to burn fuel as there is no air in space.

Front landing gear

Ejector seat
The pilot sits in an ejector seat that has fins, so that it can fly safely away from the plane.

Helium tanks
These are used for air conditioning and cooling.

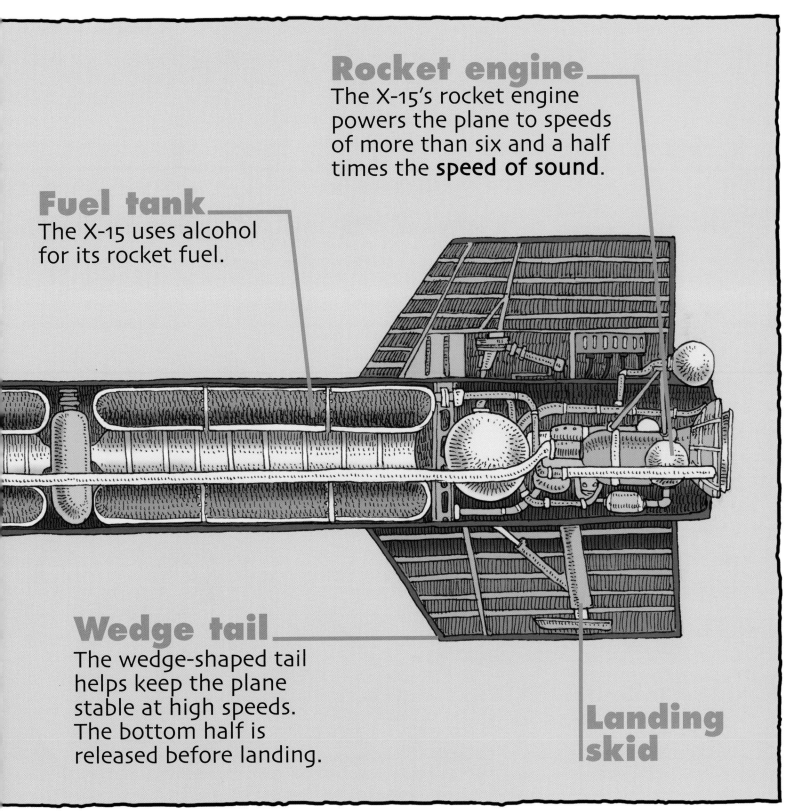

Rocket engine
The X-15's rocket engine powers the plane to speeds of more than six and a half times the **speed of sound.**

Fuel tank
The X-15 uses alcohol for its rocket fuel.

Wedge tail
The wedge-shaped tail helps keep the plane stable at high speeds. The bottom half is released before landing.

Landing skid

The Space Shuttle

The Space Shuttle was a reusable spacecraft. The Orbiter was launched into space attached to a large fuel tank and two rocket boosters. The rocket boosters dropped away and were collected to be used again. The fuel tank burnt up as it fell back to Earth. After re-entering Earth's atmosphere, the Orbiter glided back to base.

*The Space Shuttle was used to carry satellites into space as well as to repair them. Here it is launching the Hubble Space Telescope. The Shuttle was also used to ferry crew and parts to the **International Space Station**.*

The Orbiter

RCS engines
There are 44 of these small rocket engines around the Orbiter. They are used to move the Orbiter in space.

Cockpit
The Space Shuttle is flown from here. The crew controls the robotic arm from here too.

Robotic arm
This picks up the payload and positions it in space. It is also used to grab satellites for repairs.

Payload bay

Sleeping area

Nose landing gear

Toilet

Kitchen

Airlock
This allows crew with space suits to enter and exit the Orbiter in space.

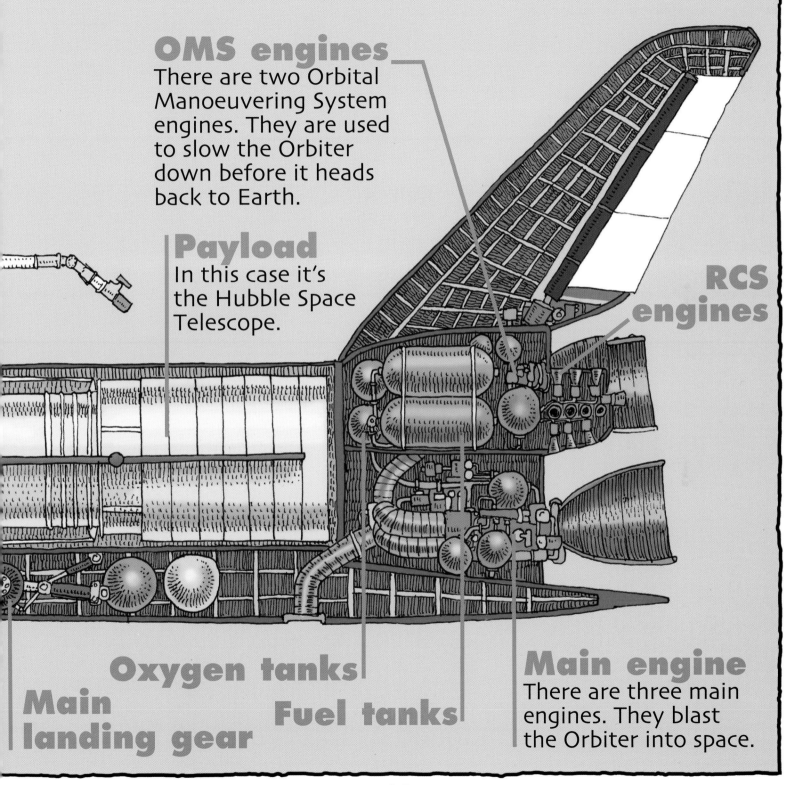

OMS engines
There are two Orbital Manoeuvering System engines. They are used to slow the Orbiter down before it heads back to Earth.

Payload
In this case it's the Hubble Space Telescope.

RCS engines

Oxygen tanks

Main landing gear

Fuel tanks

Main engine
There are three main engines. They blast the Orbiter into space.

Space Plane

The first manned, private space flight was achieved in 2004 by SpaceShipOne. It won the ten million dollar X-Prize by flying into space twice within two weeks. The first pilot, Mike Melvill, became the first astronaut to be employed by a private company.

SpaceShipOne was designed as a reusable spaceship. It was launched from its mothership, 'White Knight'. After reaching space, it re-entered Earth's atmosphere and glided back to the Mojave Air and Space Port.

SpaceShipOne

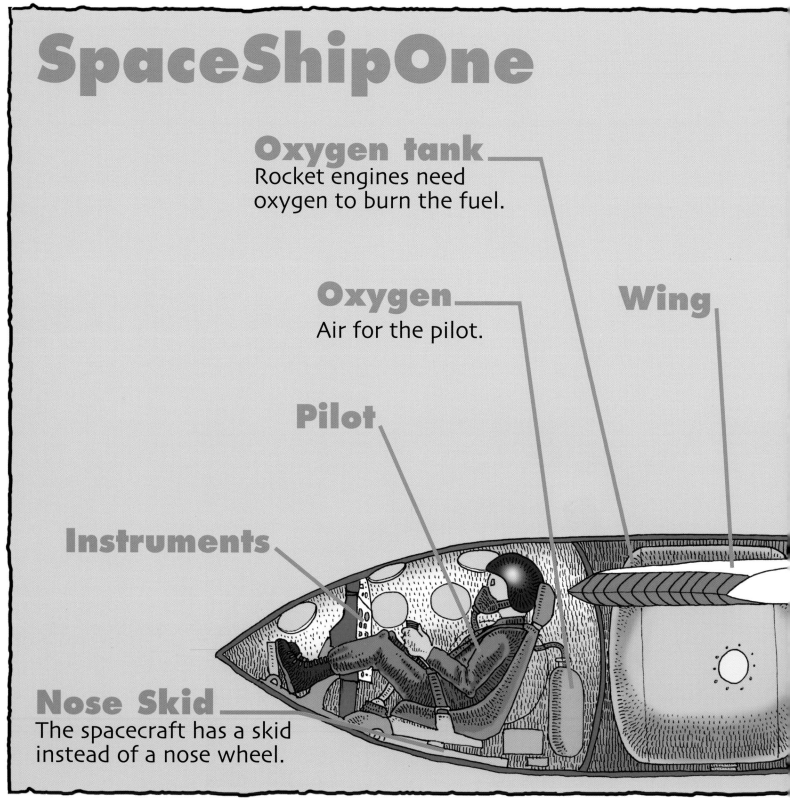

Oxygen tank
Rocket engines need oxygen to burn the fuel.

Oxygen
Air for the pilot.

Wing

Pilot

Instruments

Nose Skid
The spacecraft has a skid instead of a nose wheel.

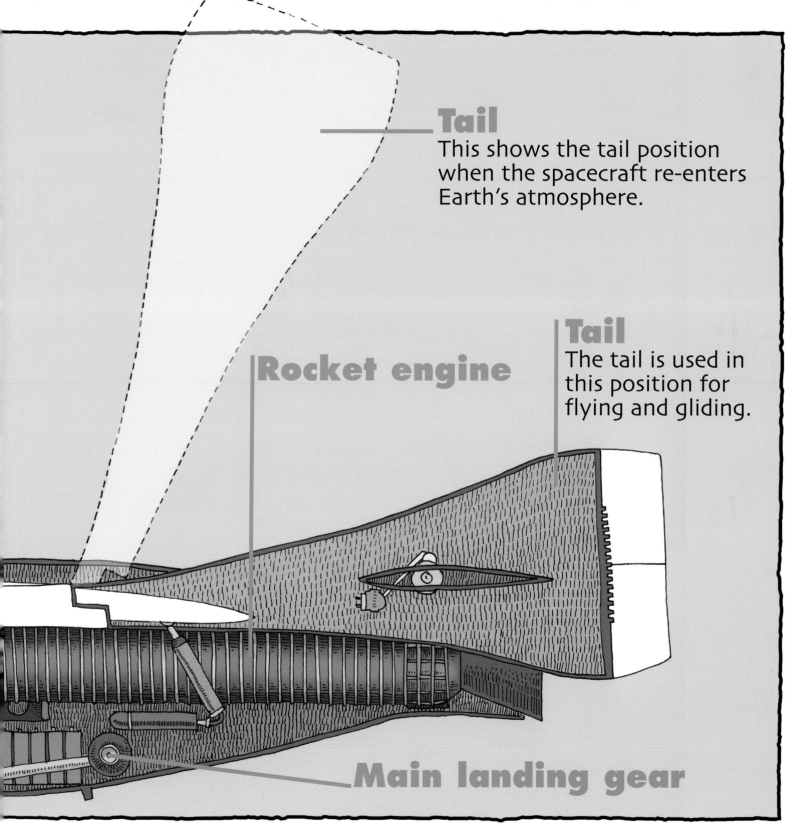

Tail
This shows the tail position when the spacecraft re-enters Earth's atmosphere.

Rocket engine

Tail
The tail is used in this position for flying and gliding.

Main landing gear

Glossary

cosmonaut
Russian version of an astronaut, meaning 'sailor of the universe'.

ejector seat
A pilot's seat in an airplane or spacecraft that can be forcibly ejected. The pilot then descends by parachute.

International Space Station
A space station in low Earth orbit. It is used as a research laboratory in which crew members from various nations conduct scientific experiments.

orbit
The path of an item in space, such as a spacecraft, as it travels around a planet, moon or star.

speed of sound
Sound travels at a speed of 1,236 kph (768 mph). Faster speeds than this are called 'supersonic'.

Index